MW01007393

# Fashion Sketchbook

## Figure Template

This Sketchbook belongs to: ________________________________________

**Lance Publishing Studio**
Lance Derrick
lancepublish.com

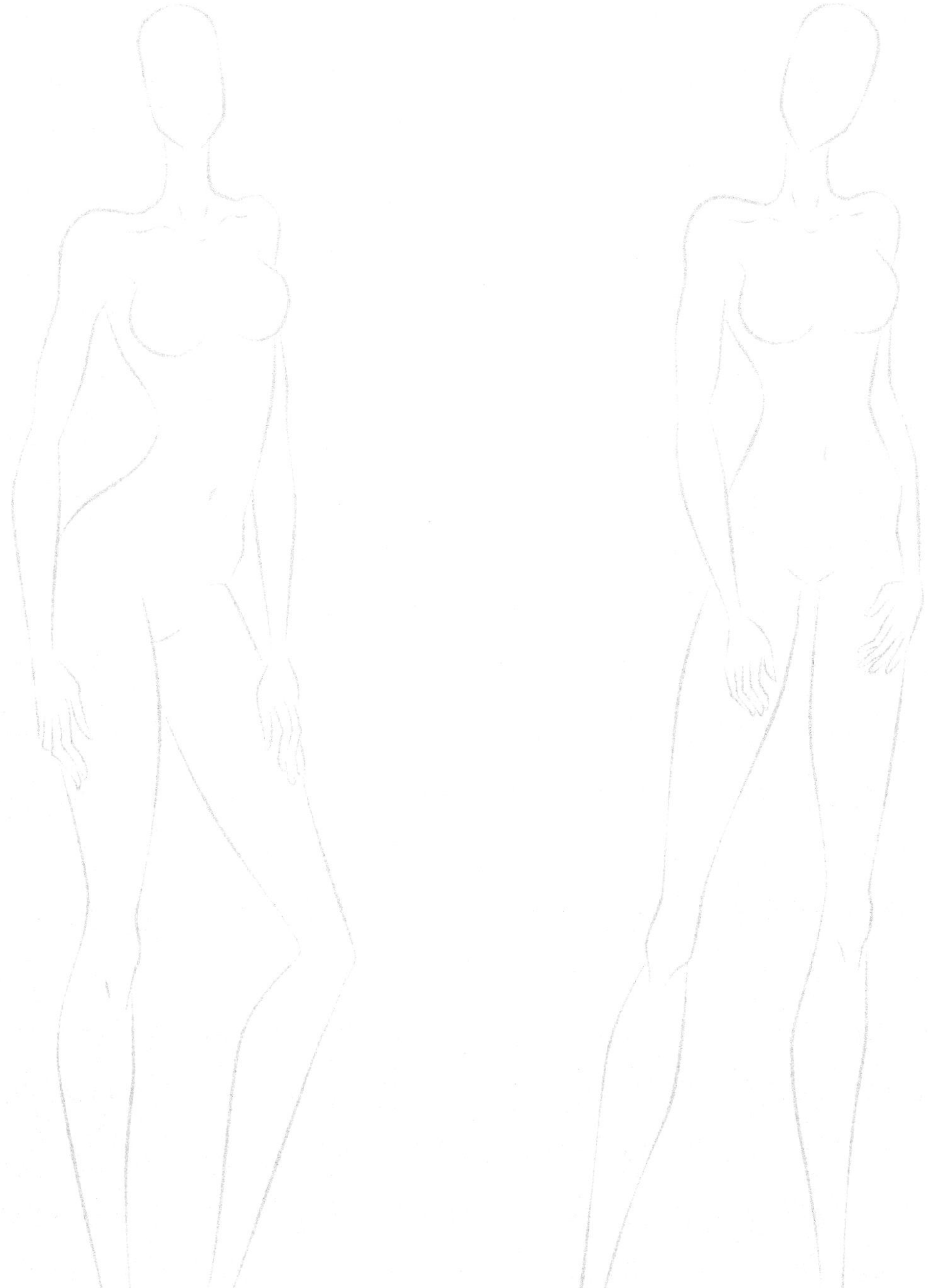

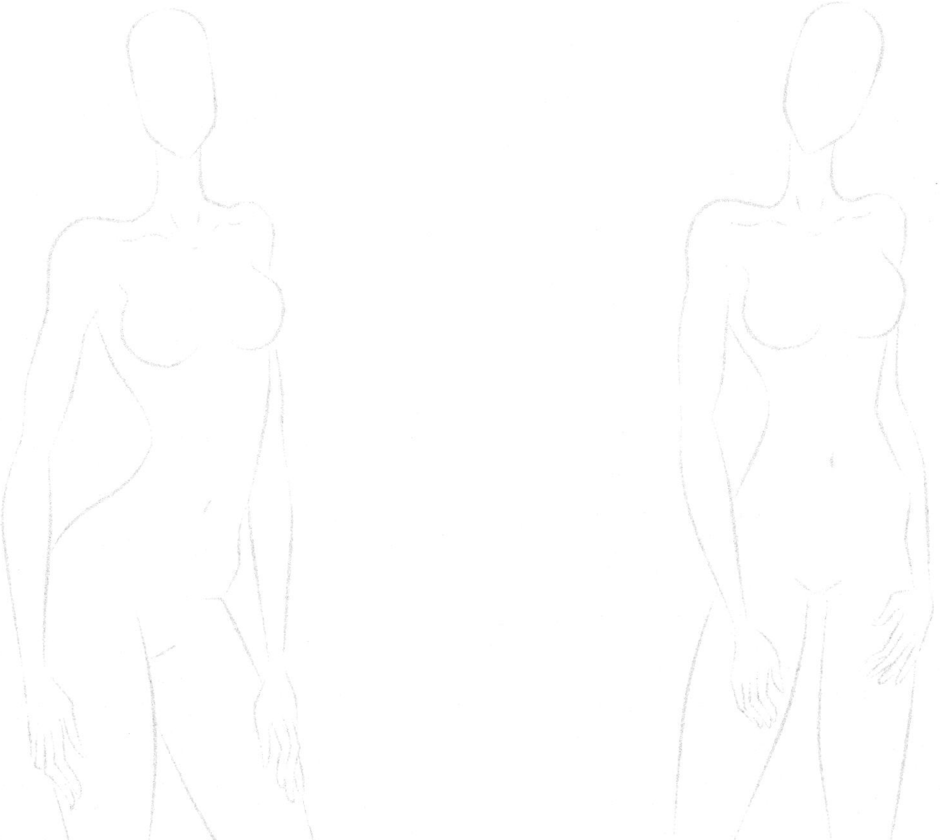

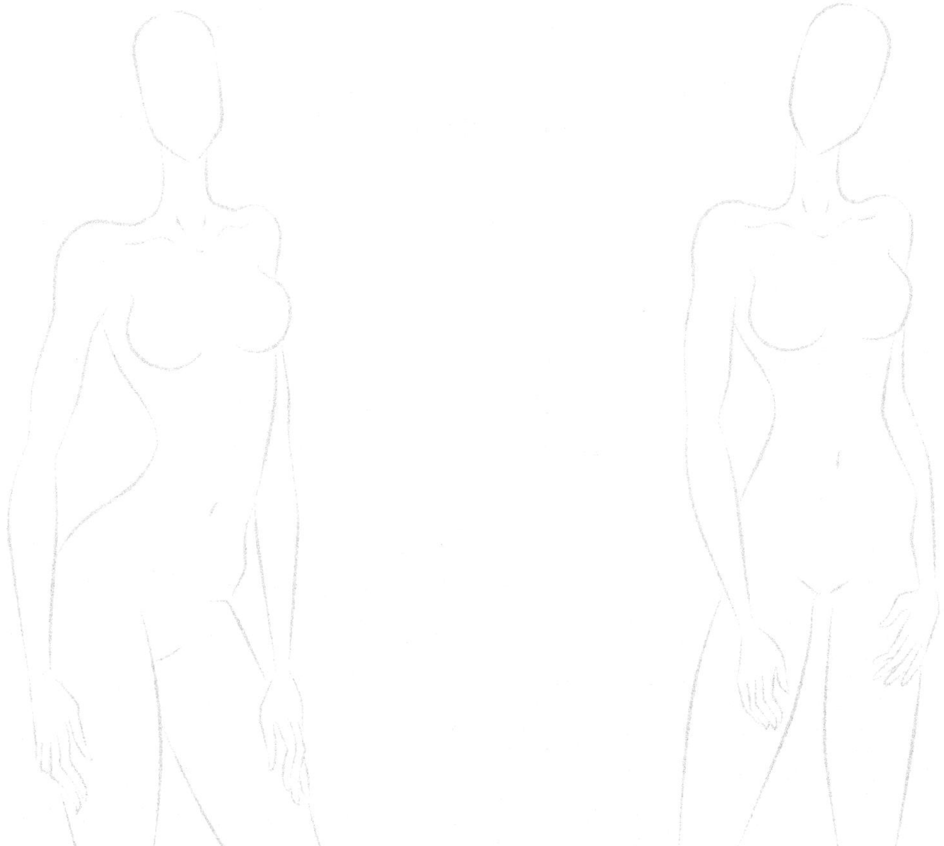

19856131R00064

Made in the USA
Middletown, DE
07 December 2018